JIM OLSON HOUSES

JIM OLSON

INTRODUCTION BY MICHAEL WEBB

THE MONACELLI PRESS

TO KATHERINE

All rights reserved. Published in the United States by The Monacelli Press,
a division of Random House, Inc., New York

The Monacelli Press is a trademark and the M design is a registered trademark of Random House, Inc.

Library of Congress Cataloging-in-Publication Data
Olson, Jim, date.
Jim Olson : houses / introduction by Michael Webb. — 1st ed.
p.   cm.
ISBN 978-1-58093-252-3
1. Olson, Jim, date. 2. Architecture, Domestic—United States. I. Title. II. Title: Houses.
NA737.O42A4   2009
720.92—dc22   2009022529

Printed in China

www.monacellipress.com

10 9 8 7 6 5 4 3 2 1
First edition

Project Editor: Matt Anderson
Project Editorial Assistant: Matt Empson
Drawings: Kendra Lundahl, Ryan Stephenson, Ryan Nace, Benjamin Hall

Designed by Think Studio, NYC

PREFACE | JIM OLSON

I live much of my life through architecture, for architecture is about life.

My two favorite places are the museum and the wilderness. Each has endless treasures to explore. I like to think of architecture as a tool that can help us look at art and nature. In both, I see infinite beauty.

Art is the expression of our humanity and our creativity. I have a visceral reaction to its many aspects—proportion, color, texture, composition, light. I try to frame these aspects with my architecture, so that others might focus on them, notice them, and feel moved by them.

Nature is a miracle that encompasses all of us—the cosmos, the sun and the planets, the sky and the sea, the trees, birds, and flowers, all the rest. Here in the Northwest, nature is benevolent, lush, and enveloping. Architecture is part of nature; it doesn't stand apart from it.

There is another attribute of art and nature that I try to incorporate into my work, an abstract spiritual quality I see in clouds moving across water, in the glow of translucent leaves lit by the sun, in the shapes of shells and rocks, and in the tactile radiance of the moon. This quality lives in the elusive light of James Turrell and the serene dark fields of Rothko, in paintings that softly blur nature's forms, like Monet's *Water Lilies* or Mary Ann Peters's murals, where details are gone but the spirit is revealed.

Architecture is always doubly faceted. It is a means of solving functional puzzles, with resolutions that make everyday life more convenient and livable. And it is a means of exploring and contemplating the beauty and mystery of life on earth and expressing the best within us. Architecture seeks the closest combination of the two.

For me, it is a quest that will last a lifetime.

ART AND NATURE:
THE LAYERED LIVING SPACES
OF JIM OLSON | MICHAEL WEBB

Creative artists find inspiration in the exceptional and in the everyday. Over the past forty years, Jim Olson's houses have been shaped by his love for Pharaonic temples and the traditional architecture of Japan, by the timeless rigor of Louis Kahn and the precision of Carlo Scarpa. He speaks with passion of his first encounter with the soaring rotunda of the Guggenheim, the interplay of light and mass in the Kimbell Art Museum, and the shadows of ancient processions between the columns of Luxor.

Olson's devotion to a select handful of architectural masterpieces is balanced by a deep attachment to the watery landscapes of Puget Sound in his native Washington. But as the architect ventures farther from his home base in Seattle—to central Colorado, Atlanta, and Rancho Mirage in southern California, to Hawaii and Hong Kong—he takes his cues from local traditions and topography. The sixteen houses and apartments featured here respond to different needs and sites, but all share a common DNA. They are the product of a singular vision and a collaborative process. They are the latest chapter in an ongoing narrative in which the houses and their owners are interwoven.

Another common thread in these projects is art. All but two of the dwellings were designed for collectors, and the best of them rival top museums in the sophistication of their interiors. The sequence of spaces, the balance of solid and void, the materials, tones, and lighting combine to enrich the experience of living with treasured works of art. Olson has encouraged clients to commission site-specific murals and installations as an integral part of the architecture, and he has done the same in his apartment on rambunctious Pioneer Square in the historic core of Seattle, which he has long shared with his wife, Katherine. The couple alternate between this richly layered space and a waterfront cabin where the colors and compositions are supplied entirely by nature.

"When I was a kid, I liked to build things all the time, and at age twelve I decided I would like to be an artist or an architect," Olson recalls. "My dad told me that if I could make my hobby my livelihood, I would always be happy." Encouraged by his mother, who had been an art major in college, and stimulated by family trips across the country, he left the rural town of his boyhood to study architecture at the University of Washington in Seattle. In the late 1950s, before Microsoft, Amazon, and Starbucks made that city a global hub, it felt cut off from the rest of America. Seattle and its huge natural harbor had flourished as a center of logging and the China trade, but the area seemed quiet and remote.

The arts flourished in this idyllic backwater. Painters such as Mark Tobey, Morris Graves, and Guy Anderson achieved widespread fame; the leading modern architects were little known beyond the region, however. After Olson graduated in 1963, he went to work for two of his local heroes: briefly for Paul Kirk and for a couple of years with Ralph Anderson, a master of daringly cantilevered wood structures. When a friend invited him to design a house, he quit his job to seize this opportunity and, in 1970, established a partnership with a former colleague from the Anderson office.

"We did a lot of nice things in the early years," says Olson, "restoring historic buildings and designing new condos, but single-family residences were always the most important. They are treasured to a much greater degree than commercial buildings, and the clients are more dependable." That is still the case. Residential commissions make up 70 percent of the billings at Olson Sundberg Kundig Allen, which the founding partner describes as "a larger firm that feels small. It's a very cooperative place—we critique each other all the time. Tom [Kundig] and I have our own little worlds within it, and clients often check our web site to decide who they would like to work with." Each architect has a distinct language and nurtures productive dialogues with owners, colleagues, and frequent collaborators.

The process usually begins with a call and a follow-up meeting. The clients describe their interests and present lists and clippings to identify their preferences and dislikes. Some have a clear picture of what they want, others are more concerned with how it will work. If the chemistry is right, architect and clients start discussing goals and budgets, looking at what's been built in the neighborhood, and socializing over dinner. For Olson, the goal is to get to know the clients as well as they know each other and establish a bond. It's going to be a close, three-year relationship that will be tested repeatedly as choices are made and the house takes shape.

Before he starts designing, the architect immerses himself in the history and geography of the area, especially if he has not built there before. He looks at older buildings that have worn well, makes field trips to learn about the local vernacular, and tries to visit the clients' favorite structures, wherever they may be. Most importantly, he spends many hours on the site, making notes of where the sun rises and sets and the direction of the prevailing wind. He fills notebooks with sketches and diagrams in a quest for the ideal orientation and the proper framing of the views. That research feeds into subsequent meetings with the clients and helps them consider alternative solutions.

"I try not to lock in too early," says Olson, "and to avoid that, I'll sometimes sketch as many as fifteen different options. I may go back to my first idea, but I've given other possibilities a chance. When I take in a lot of information, things start popping pretty fast." He picks a colleague to be project manager and start fleshing out his concept. Ideas are challenged in office critiques and fed into a computer so that the design can be viewed in three dimensions and translated into little wood or paper models. "I continue to make sketches and meet with the clients every two or three weeks for months," Olson says. "Their reactions vary. The design gets increasingly detailed and I remain at the heart of the project until it's finished, supervising the choice of colors, materials, furniture, and the smallest details."

Olson approaches every commission in a similar way, but each one presents a fresh challenge and an invitation to try something new. In contrast to architects who market a brand image and play variations on one or two themes, he tailors each house to the clients' needs and intangible desires, to climate, landscape, or urban grain, and to the owners' collections. Each represents a different set of opportunities and constraints, and they have to be delicately balanced.

Context can be a decisive factor. When a commission came from a couple in a historic neighborhood of Atlanta, Olson studied books on antebellum mansions and rented a copy of *Gone with the Wind* to immerse himself in the myths of the South. The pedimented facade of the Modern Antebellum House flaunts a gutsy steel I-beam, and the tightly coiled oval stair has a balustrade inspired by a classic house in Savannah. Tradition is given a contemporary spin. In Rancho Mirage, the rugged landscape inspired the sand-toned Desert House, which nestles amid boulders and offers protection from the searing heat and glare of summer. A blank wall shuts out neighbors in this suburban development, and deep-set windows frame stunning vistas of the mountains.

These houses are site-specific; elsewhere, Olson had greater freedom to indulge his clients' wishes. The Lake House in Seattle was built for descendents of the family that commissioned Erich Mendelsohn to design sleek department stores in Weimar Germany and a library in Jerusalem. They wanted to pay homage to the modern master with a rounded wall; the architect gave them a sensuously curved plane, clad in metal shingles and topped with a prismatic skylight by artist Ed Carpenter that casts a shimmering veil of light across the living room.

For a project on the big island of Hawaii, the client sketched three pavilions—for living, sleeping, and guests—and assembled a thick stack of images that linked this concept to the residential compounds of southeast Asia. Olson took his wife to Bali to experience first-hand the processional sequence of pavilions and courtyards, and incorporated this sense of intimacy into the Ocean House. Jutting roofs and walls provide shelter from the elements, and reflecting pools mirror sky and plantings.

Though Olson signs his name in a variety of ways, there has been a consistency in the quality of his work and his use of favorite features over a span of forty years. Natural materials and soft tones are a constant. Another is the manipulation of light. He often employs projecting roofs and "eyebrows"— jutting ledges that bounce sunlight and give high-ceilinged rooms a human scale. He conceals the edges of large windows so that the glass becomes invisible and occupants are transported outside to a vista of mountains, a city garden, or islands in the Pacific. The "infinite ceiling," a foglike effect produced in a shallow recess with rounded edges, was inspired by the perceptual artworks of James Turrell and is a highlight of several houses and apartments.

Strong axes bring order to the larger houses, and columns articulate the broad concourses of an American Place and the House of Light. Olson designed both at the same time in the same city for collectors who were friends, and he had to keep them from looking too alike, even though their size and program were similar. He achieved this in the siting. An American Place weaves among the trees, deferring to the lake it borders, while the House of Light is a single stand-alone pavilion. Olson sees similarities between these projects and his own modest retreats. "I like small cozy spaces, and I try to incorporate them into the grandest houses," he says. "People are people; they may need expansive areas for displaying art or entertaining, but not for their personal creature comforts."

Sustainability is an issue that engaged Olson long before it became an urgent concern for a broad public. The Earth House, an early project, has a grass-covered roof and was designed to heat and cool itself. A heat chimney at the Lake House draws cool air in at the base and vents it at the top. The Hong Kong Villa is ten times the size of the owners' previous residence, but their energy bill has declined. The traditional devices of cross-ventilation, sun baffles, and thermal mass have become routine. Many clients are now demanding green houses that go beyond the passive strategies of the past and are willing to invest in photovoltaic panels and geothermal heating and cooling systems. The architect is happy to explore new ways to reduce the carbon footprint, but as he observes, "you can learn a lot from how people built before modern technologies were introduced."

As a boy, Olson spent much of his time in the woods, and nature is still a commanding presence in his world. He likes to knit his houses into the landscape rather than set them apart. The Bird Watchers' House in Washington stacks three glass cubes at the edge of a forest. That reduces the footprint of the house and gives the owners a multilevel belvedere from which to observe birds on the ground and in the treetops. Reflections in the glass dematerialize the house, and a solid stair core provides sheltered places for small works of art. Another couple bought an exposed, high-altitude site in the farming country of eastern Oregon and asked the architect for an old-fashioned barn plus his version of Philip Johnson's Glass House. Having worked as scientists, they wanted to immerse themselves in the rhythms of rural life. Olson picked up on the local vernacular of barns with gambrel roofs and gave a jaunty tilt to the main house. The wooden barn is an organic extension of the landscape; the Glass Farmhouse is its crystalline companion.

On occasion, Olson calls on a landscape architect to mediate between building and nature. Charles Anderson took the horizontal lines of the House of Light and extended them in the form of a cascading staircase. Kathryn Gustafson echoed the curved wall of the Lake House in low concrete retaining walls that radiate out like ripples in a pond. Both are seamless collaborations that make it hard to see where the work of one designer ends and another begins.

Sitting on the deck of his cabin by Puget Sound, where plantings swallow up the steel-and-timber frame, Olson can reflect on his next project. It's no surprise that collectors gravitate toward him, for he has an intuitive understanding of their needs. "Art tells you more about the client than they would ever say in words," he observes. "I become emotionally involved with some of the paintings and feel I'm designing the house for them as well as the owner." In planning an American Place, he researched individual artists in books and museums and made scale copies of every work in the collection, which has been exhibited in the National Gallery of Art in Washington, D.C.

The demands of these artworks varied according to their size and the natural affinities that draw one to another. The product of this painstaking research is a hierarchy of installations, ranging from the Gaston Lachaise bronze nude silhouetted in an opening to the lake, on axis with the entry, to the four small masterpieces (by Jackson Pollock, Edward Hopper, Arshile Gorky, and John Marin) in the owner's intimate study. For each, the natural and task lighting was meticulously calibrated so that the works are seen to best advantage at every time of day.

On an entirely different scale, the Glass Apartment in Seattle is designed to set off the owner's collection of work by Dale Chihuly and his peers as well as Native American and Asian art. Olson picked up on the circles and shells that are a recurrent motif of those cultures and transmuted them into free-form translucent panels that catch the light and evoke the fluidity of water.

The Zen House was designed as a calming retreat for a high-profile businessman. Olson treated the approach as a decompression chamber: a layered sequence of courtyards and pebbled pathways leads to the entry and—in a dramatic revelation just inside the main entry—a panoramic view across the water to downtown Seattle. The feeling of release created here is heightened by a mural along the inner wall: a subtly toned abstraction by Mary Ann Peters, a local artist whose work evokes the mist-shrouded skies over Puget Sound. Olson also put her together with the entrepreneur who commissioned the expansive Hong Kong Villa on an unspoiled shore of that tropical island. Commuting home from the concrete jungle of the business district, the owner thrilled to the spectacle of hawks circling over the verdant jungle flanking the road. That inspired the artist to create a contemporary version of an ink-wash scroll on both sides of a long gallery. It suggests what the hawks might see as they soar through the air, and it is as tenderly evocative of the natural world as Monet's linear canvases of water lilies.

Olson's concern for art is matched by his involvement with every aspect of the interiors. Like the architects of the Arts and Crafts movement and the pioneer modernists, from Mackintosh and Wright to Mies, he strives to make his houses a seamless whole. It's a rare skill among contemporary architects, but Olson never dictates decor as his paternalistic forbears did. Where Wright loved to dominate, Olson seeks to persuade. "When I'm sketching a floor plan, I draw in furniture to give me a sense of scale, and as an extension of the architecture," he remarks. "I think of it as a design problem—what does it have to do, where is it going to be, and what does it relate to?" Some clients prefer to hire their own interior designer, and that often turns out to be Terry Hunziker—especially in the Northwest. He works in perfect harmony with Olson and adds another level of refinement and style.

It is this sensitivity to clients and collaborators that gives Olson's houses their livability and understated beauty. The intangible feel as much as the look is what delights their owners. Large and small, in town and country, these houses are rooted in the land yet seem to float free, framing art and nature, affording spaces for celebration and contemplation.

July 3, 2002 Longbranch/cabin 7:55 PM cabin
cloudy & cool — I've been working on
addition today — in plan & elev. — w
should it look like in 3D — ?

quick — what is the point here? —
what is important? a composition of
layers made up of sticks — &
floating planes — I think it should be
black — then I flip/flop to driftwood &
& it layers w/ the trees in the woods —

OLSON CABIN | **LONGBRANCH, WASHINGTON** 1959, 1981, 1997, 2003

A century ago, my grandparents built a second home on a forested waterfront site. The house was destroyed by fire, and over the past fifty years, I have created a modestly scaled retreat for three generations of my own family. The first new building, a fourteen-foot-square bunkhouse, was planned to accommodate guests. In 1981, a tiny bedroom and bathroom and, more recently, a lofty living/guest room and deck were added; these double the square footage of the earlier elements. The structure recedes into the woods, deferring to the natural beauty of the landscape. It also chronicles the evolution of residential architecture in the Northwest, from simple post-and-beam construction to airy geometries that expand to capture light and space.

The galvanized steel columns and laminated wood beams of the addition frame an invisible wall of glass opening onto an unspoiled shore and a clear view across Puget Sound. The floor plane is extended so that the addition looks into the treetops and hovers above the sandy beach. New and old spaces are tightly knitted together and plainly furnished.

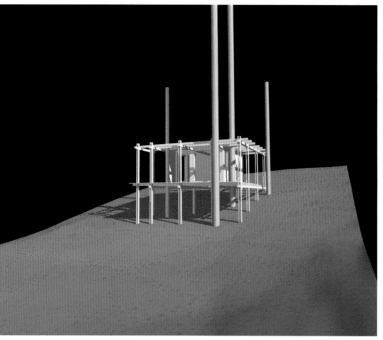 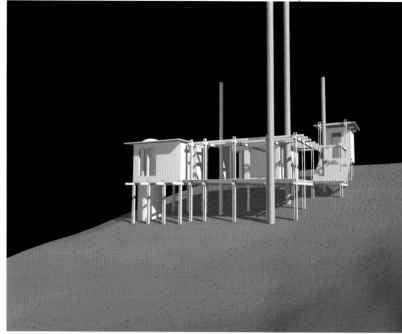

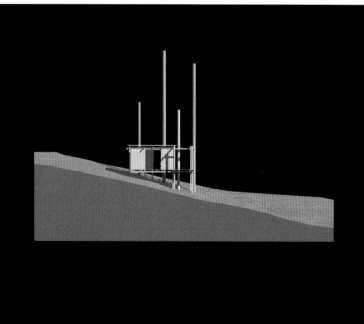 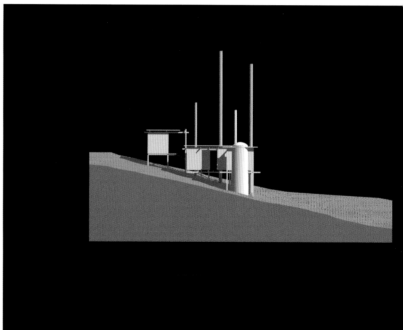

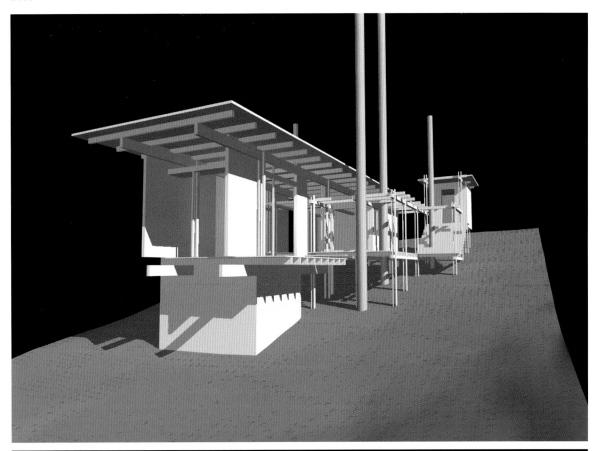

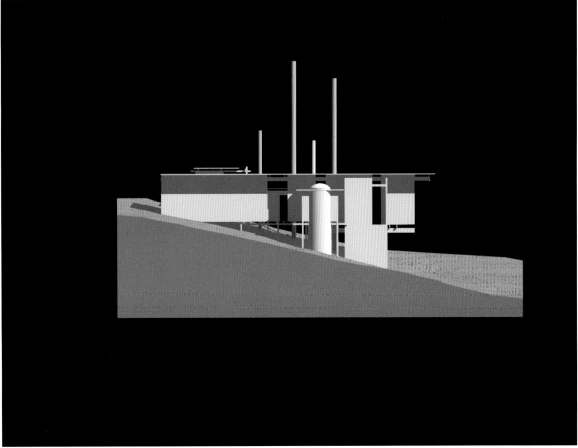

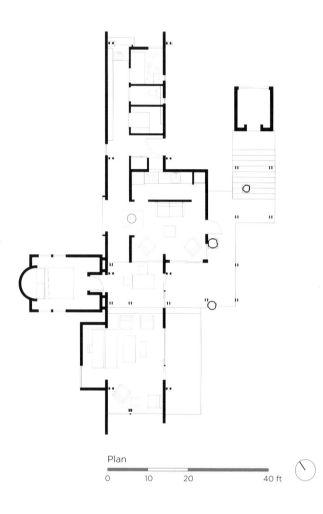

Plan

0   10   20   40 ft

DESERT HOUSE

RANCHO MIRAGE, CALIFORNIA 1999

A two-hour drive from Los Angeles, Palm Springs was first developed as a winter resort and a showcase of modernism through the 1950s, but after the advent of air conditioning, it was transformed into a twenty-mile sprawl of generic suburban developments. The Desert House recaptures the freshness of the first settlement. It is located on a ridge above an arroyo in a community that preserves the natural beauty of rocks and mountains and gives each plot a sense of privacy.

Natural materials—concrete, stone, stucco, and wood—blend with the earth tones of the surroundings. Broad overhangs provide shade yet allow the winter sun to warm the house, and the mass of the construction moderates the extremes of temperature. Two offset colonnades outside the living areas augment the interiors, and a cylindrical breakfast room with glass doors plays against the rectilinear facade. A central circulation spine, topped by a clerestory that diffuses natural light, extends from the entry to a garden plaza and reflecting pool. Generous public and more intimate private rooms open from this concourse, and the soft tones of walls and furnishings blend house and desert.

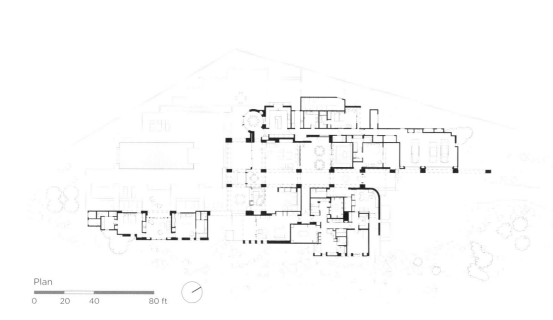

Plan

0   20   40   80 ft

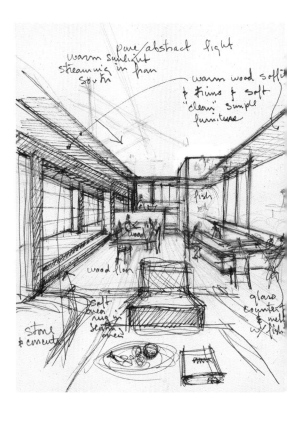

ZEN HOUSE | SEATTLE, WASHINGTON 1999

Designed as a tranquil retreat for a busy executive, this house steps down a bluff overlooking Elliott Bay and downtown Seattle. It is concealed from the street by high walls and is rotated to face the bay. Concrete walls enclose small courtyards and portals; a pebbled path leads through these layered spaces and into a long, spacious living room lined on one side with expansive windows that frame the city across the water. A terrace opens from one corner of the room; at the far end is an open kitchen that is raised a foot above the dining area and a bar. The space is well suited for entertaining friends.

The indirect approach and the woodsy feel of the interior evoke the spirit of Japan. White oak floors and fir joinery warm the living room, and the striking view to the east is balanced by an atmospheric mural by artist Mary Ann Peters that covers the inner wall. Tying together the space is a shallow vaulted ceiling with cove lighting—a design inspired by the luminous works of James Turrell. Beyond is the master suite and home office. Steps lead down to guest rooms, fitness space, and media center on the lower level.

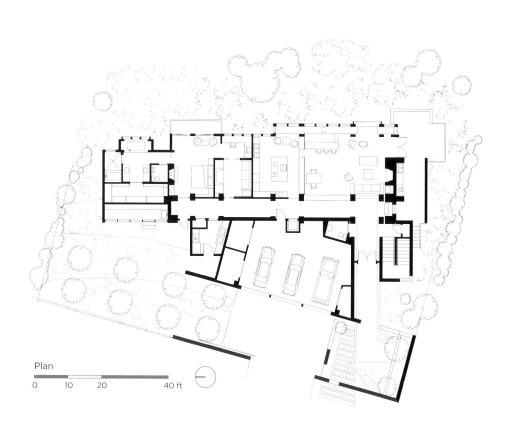

Plan

0   10   20   40 ft

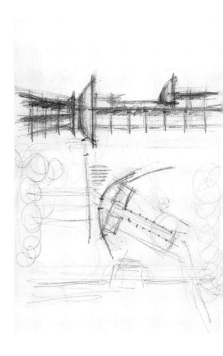

LAKE HOUSE | **MERCER ISLAND, WASHINGTON** 2004

This house on the shore of Lake Washington is a fusion of art, nature, and sustainable design. It is oriented to respond to the path of the sun, prevailing winds, and existing shade trees in order to achieve cross-ventilation and passive solar gain. The siting allows the owners to open the house to courtyards and terraces, views over the water, and the garden. The flat roof is planted with hardy succulents. Complementing the salvaged redwood facing of the two-story facade is a dramatically curved screen wall shingled in Rheinzink alloy. It looks back to the signature curves of Erich Mendelsohn, who designed department stores for the owners' family in the 1920s.

The curving plane catches the morning sun as it hits the south facade, drawing it into the house and through a skylight where the roof meets the wall. A dichroic glass sculpture by artist Ed Carpenter, suspended just below the skylight, projects colored light that traces the sun's arc across the wall. At opposite ends of the rectilinear plan are a central kitchen that allows flexibility in dining indoors or out, a book-lined study, and bedrooms for the owners and guests.

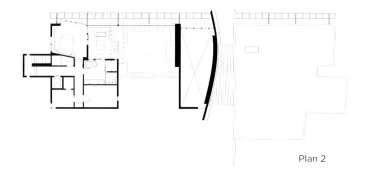

Plan 2

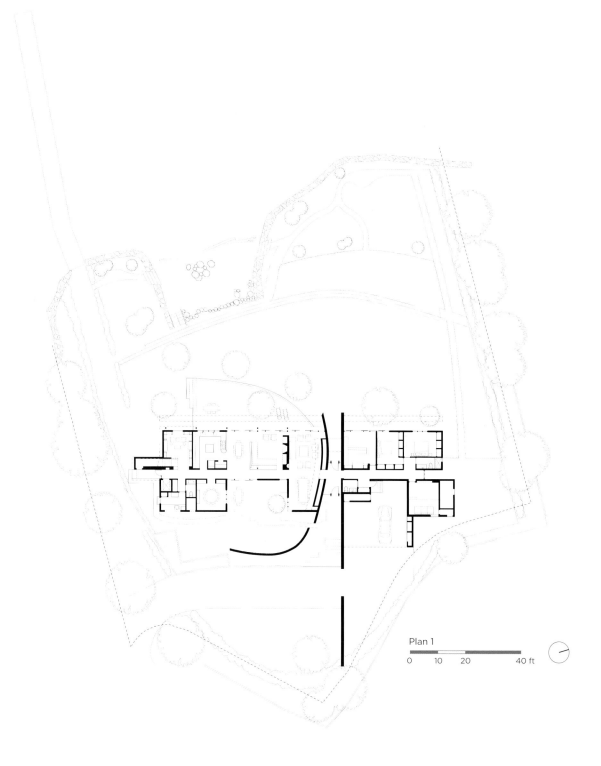

Plan 1

0   10   20   40 ft

BIRD WATCHERS' HOUSE | **MAPLE VALLEY, WASHINGTON** 2002

Located in a rural area south of Seattle, on a boundary between forest and meadow, this three-story house was designed for two avid ornithologists. Window walls, rooftop terraces, and small outdoor buildings allow nature to be experienced close-up and in every direction. The verticality of the structure, a stack of glass boxes, minimizes the impact on the site and provides vantage points for observing birds both at ground level and in the treetops.

The cross-axial plan is oriented to the cardinal directions, dividing the house into four corner blocks. However, its massing is irregular, suggesting the interlocking volumes of a Rubik's Cube. At the center of the house is a skylit "cosmic" shaft, a symbolic link between earth and sky; the owners display their collection of small paintings in this light-filtering core. The wood-framed structure is partially covered with metal and shotcrete. The entrance is defined by a tall gridded wall set behind a curving partition on which is mounted Philip McCracken's bronze *Bird in Flight*. Atop the second story is an inhabitable roof garden with a greenhouse and vegetable garden.

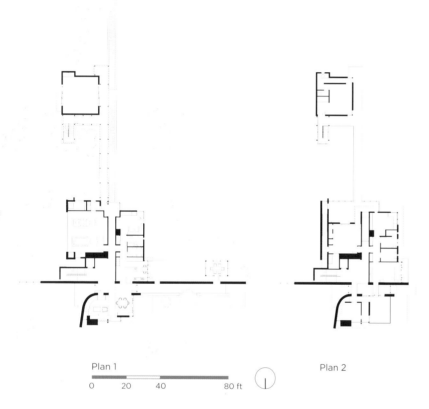

Plan 1

0   20   40   80 ft

Plan 2

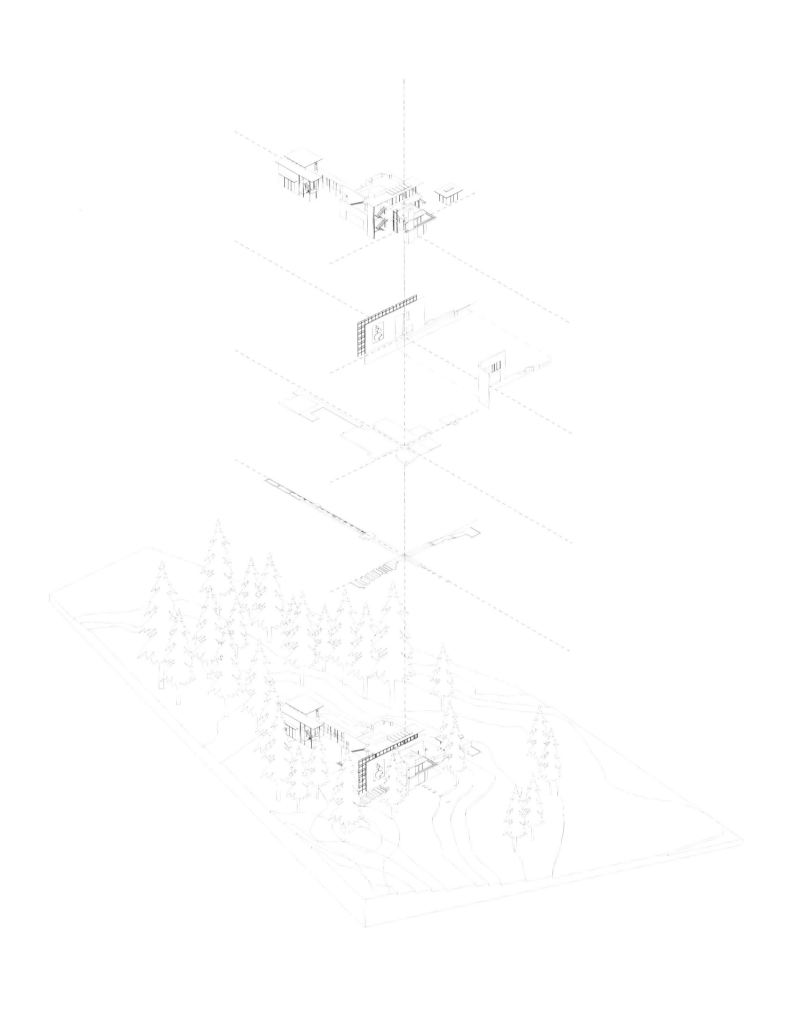

note — let end of Living on water side
be a bay that expands out
other side (south) is confined by
side walls —

MODERN ANTEBELLUM HOUSE | **ATLANTA, GEORGIA** 2004

Palladian villas inspired the columns and pediments of the traditional houses and plantations that define the Southern states. The Modern Antebellum House, located in a historic residential neighborhood of Atlanta, reinterprets the regional vernacular with modern materials. A steel I-beam braces a tall portico of precast concrete columns; climbing vines soften the structure's raw quality. The side walls are blank—the lot is narrow—and red sandstone cladding evokes the traditional brick. In contrast, the street and garden facades are fully glazed to open the house to lush landscaping.

The plan draws on the symmetry and linear sequences of traditional models. A three-story ovoid staircase, inspired by that of the landmark Isaiah Davenport house in Savannah, links the basement parking level to the upstairs bedrooms. The coved ceiling over the staircase is haint blue—a color traditionally used to scare away ghosts. Hidden clerestory windows pull in natural light and can be opened to evacuate hot air. The subtle palette and sensuous textures of interior designer Terry Hunziger enrich the simple materials and soaring great room.

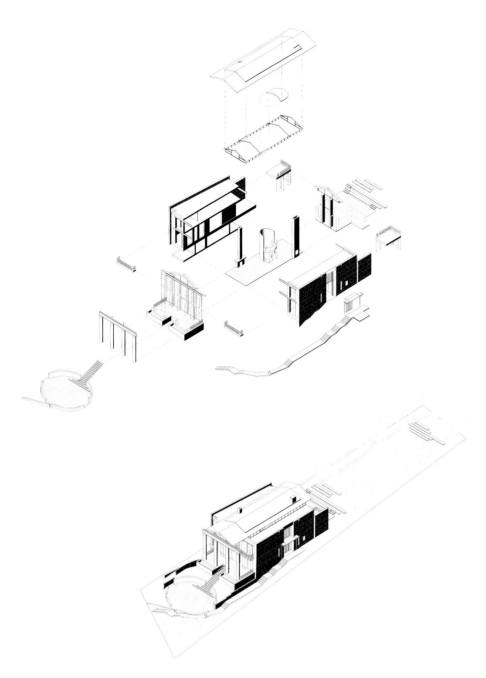

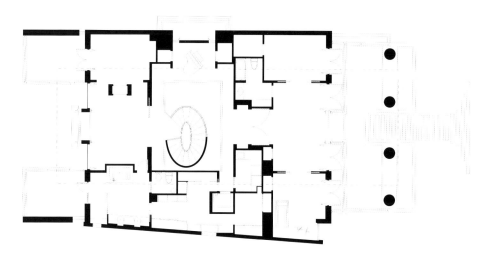

Plan 2

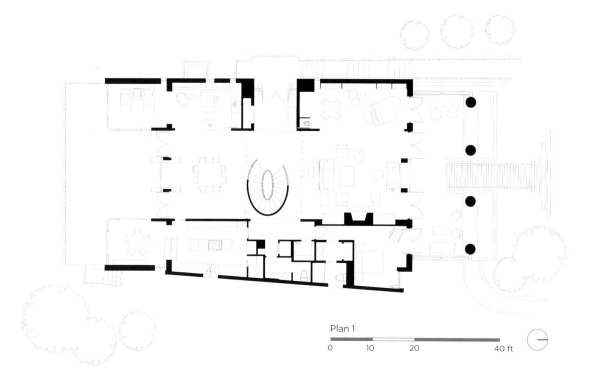

Plan 1

0   10   20   40 ft

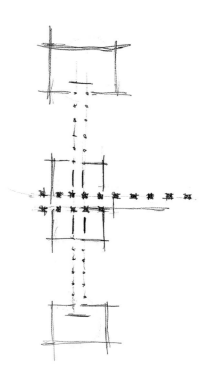

AN AMERICAN PLACE |

This understated house on the east shore of Lake Washington defers both to its wooded site and to one of the nation's premier collections of modern American art. The linear structure steps delicately among the trees while giving every room a view of the water. Portuguese limestone and stained cedar soften the concrete-and-steel structure, and their subtle tones are an integral part of the landscape. Shallow-pitched eaves hover over the long, low facade like those of a traditional Japanese house.

A lofty hall extends from the steel-and-wood entry canopy through the center of the house to a glass wall that frames a view of the lake and silhouettes a massive bronze nude by Gaston Lachaise. Cutting across this hall is a lengthy gallery leading from a study and master suite at the north through spacious reception areas to a glass bridge; the bridge connects to the upper level of a two-story guest house, which sits in a gully to the south. The house was scaled to heighten the impact of the collection. Natural light is carefully balanced, and the paintings are unobtrusively protected from direct sun. Creature comforts are also present—notably in the glass-enclosed shower that juts into a walled Japanese garden.

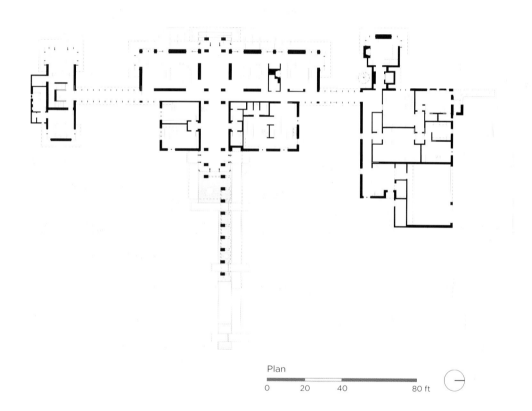

Plan

0   20   40   80 ft

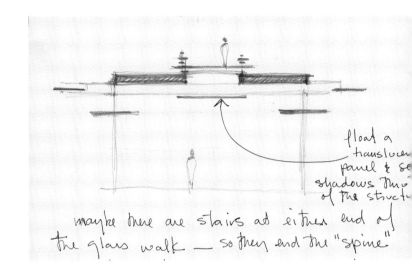

float a
translucen
panel & se
shadows thro
of the structu

maybe there are stairs at either end of
the glass walk — so they end the "spine"

HOUSE OF LIGHT | SEATTLE, WASHINGTON 2005

A couple commissioned this wood, steel, and glass house on the shore of Lake Washington as a place to display their collection of contemporary art and to entertain fellow enthusiasts. On the landward side, the site is anchored by a 130-foot-long sculpture by Richard Serra. On the lake side, reflecting pools step down from the facade, mediating between the house and the water. A slatted metal canopy shades the interior from direct sun, while allowing glimpses of the sky through large spans of glass. Buffalo grass on the flat roof and trellises with hanging vines integrate the house and garden.

Major artworks are installed in a two-story, top-lighted gallery—the luminous spine of the house—and in the airy rooms to either side. Natural illumination from a linear skylight and clerestories is filtered through a transparent fabric scrim at ceiling level. At the east end of the gallery is a site-specific installation by James Turrell, a skyspace illuminated by LEDs. Throughout the house, a strong sense of axiality and order prevails. Public rooms for entertaining lead into each other at the center of the plan, while informal and intimate rooms are located to either end of the gallery, with bedrooms on the second level.

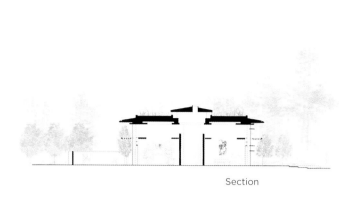

Section

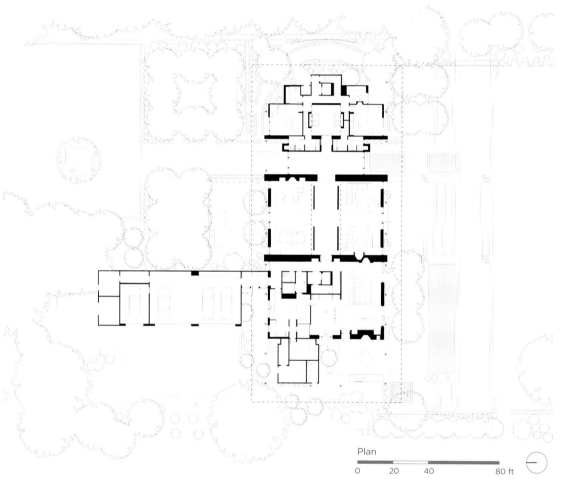

Plan

0   20   40   80 ft

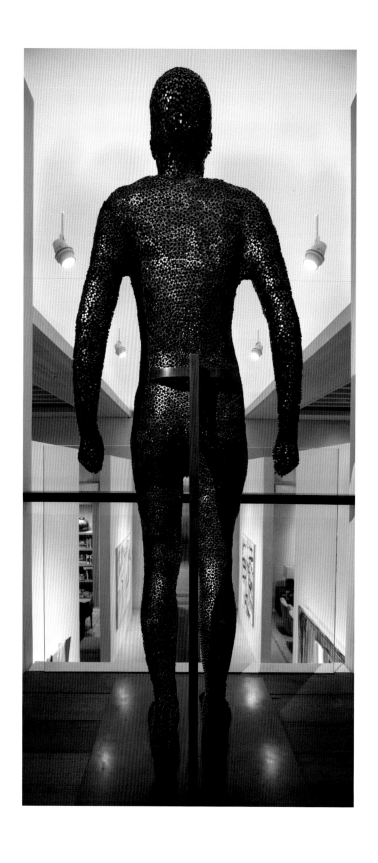

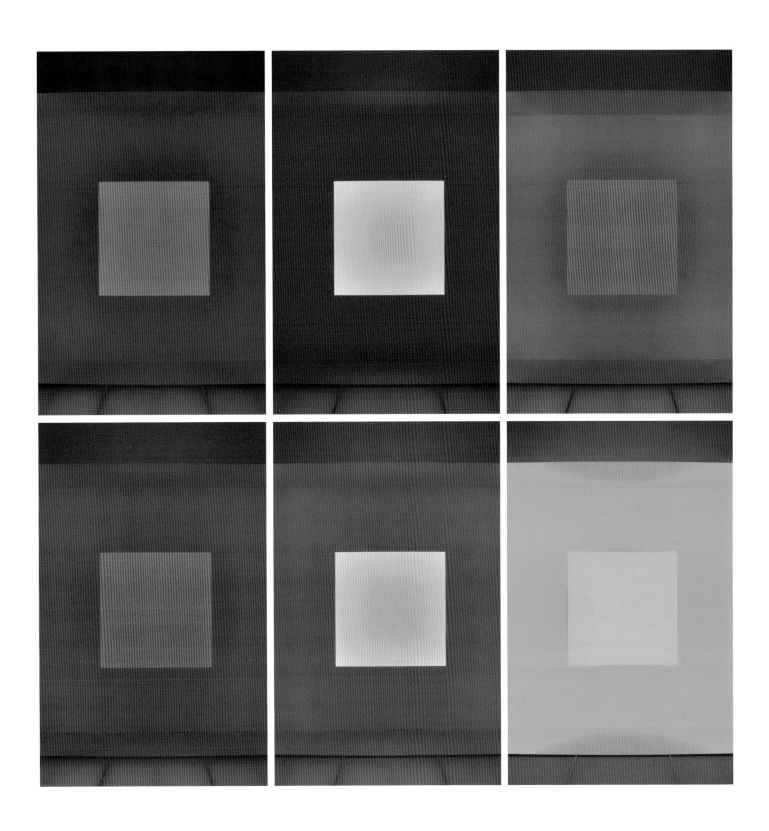

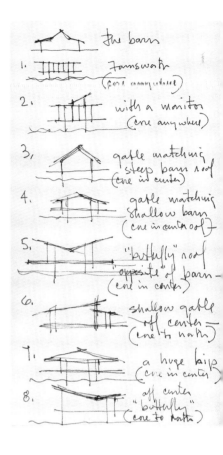

GLASS FARMHOUSE | EASTERN OREGON 2008

Surrounded by wheat fields on a high-altitude plateau stand a small glass house and a solid, traditional barn. The owners, inspired by Philip Johnson's Glass House, wanted a refuge that opens up to the prairie and mountains. The structures are conveniently close to each other and enjoy a sense of isolation at the end of a long country road. The roof of the wood-frame barn, which houses farm equipment below and guest rooms above, was inspired by the local vernacular and is echoed in the shed roof of the glass house.

Three sides of the house consist of high-efficiency glass framed with steel; on the north is a solid exterior wall. Inside the transparent shell, living, eating, and sleeping areas surround an enclosure that contains the bathroom, study, and storage. The house rests on a concrete slab supported on a concrete foundation. In this way, the heat-absorbing and -releasing thermal mass is isolated from the ground plane. The window system combines transparency with energy-efficiency. Heat loss and gain is managed largely by the orientation of the house: on the south side, an eyebrow, or light shelf, deflects midday summer sun but admits low-angle winter sunlight.

Plan

0   20   40   80 ft

TRANSPARENT LOFT | SEATTLE, WASHINGTON 2007

This eighteenth-floor condominium in downtown Seattle carries the idea of transparency to its logical extreme. The goal was to improve the boxy proportions of a speculative apartment, giving it the openness of a converted loft. The kitchen and master bathroom are enclosed with walls of glass to match the expanses of glazing on two of the exterior facades and around the recessed terrace. The elevation of the apartment assures privacy, as does the separation of public and private areas with a wall and sliding screen. Rolling blinds can be lowered to protect artworks from glare. When the blinds are raised, especially at night, the city skyline provides a thrilling, three-dimensional mural.

The interior design is minimal in material and palette. A polished black floor sets off the glass and white walls and is warmed by wood tables, paneling, and casework and the soft tones of upholstered seating, installed by interior designer Ted Tuttle. In the bathroom, mirrors mounted on the glass walls feel suspended in space; the same illusion is presented by metal fittings and sleek cabinets in the kitchen. The decor provides a neutral backdrop for the owners' collection of life-sized sculptural figures and minimalist paintings.

Plan

0   10   20   40 ft

CITY APARTMENT | **SEATTLE, WASHINGTON** 2008

Located in downtown Seattle's Millennium Tower, this duplex apartment looks out to a forest of high-rises. The striking vistas are complemented by the tactile and serene interiors. The owners, who previously lived in a large, suburban house, wanted to retain their accustomed ease and comfort in this smaller city apartment. Clean modern lines and a warm wood palette instill tranquility, augment the space, and provide an appropriate setting for a collection of contemporary paintings and sculptures. Privacy and light are controlled by moving panels of translucent glass suspended from a ceiling track. Interior designer Holly McKinley designed furniture pieces that harmonize with the architecture.

The apartment is bisected by a niche-filled partition of anigre wood that provides a display wall for small sculptures and art objects and animates the surrounding space. The niches are lit with translucent Plexiglas panels, which produce a soft glow. Kitchen and family room are separated by a hearth yet are open to one another. Public and service spaces are located on the main level, and upstairs are private rooms, including the master suite, guest suite, and soundproofed media room.

Plan 2

Plan 1

0   10   20   40 ft

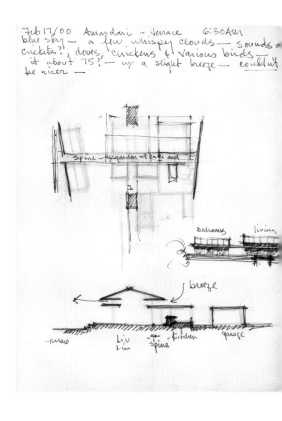

OCEAN HOUSE | HAWAII ISLAND, HAWAII 2003

Inspired by traditional Balinese palaces and temples, the Ocean House, near Mauna Kea in Hawaii, is located on a promontory of exposed lava. Three pavilions and their connecting pathways rest on a poured concrete foundation; lava rock was replaced around it to integrate the house with the striking natural landscape. Lush tropical plantings and dramatic lighting weave together the landscape and the indoor and outdoor living spaces.

The pavilions, contained within a walled compound, have broad roof overhangs. The master suite is set at an angle along the southern boundary and appears to float like a boat toward a shoreline promontory. The pavilions containing the living areas and guest suites are linked by cross-axial galleries. These axes are strengthened by a series of reflecting pools, culminating in an outdoor pool that merges into the watery horizon. All of the rooms and walkways open onto courtyards, which shelter delicate plants from wind and sun.

The owner collects traditional Asian sculpture and minimalist modern art. These works are set off by the bare spans of concrete and stone and the rich accents of teak and bronze. The visually rich materials withstand the assault of sun and sea air.

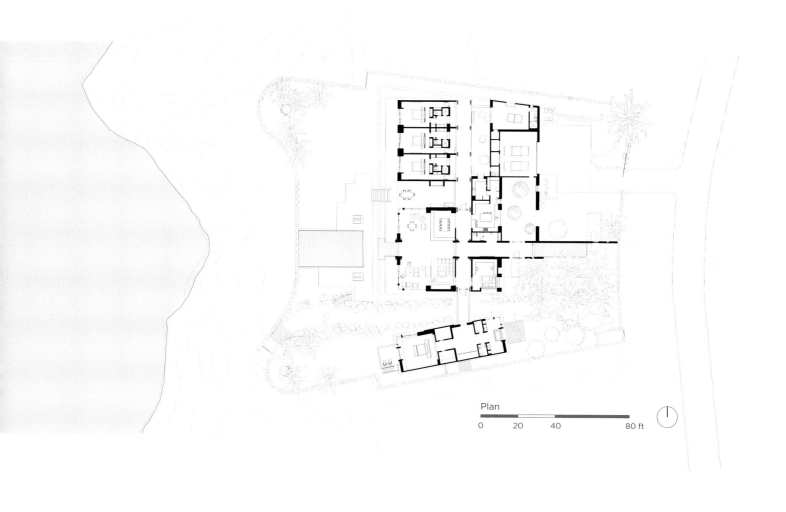

Plan

0   20   40   80 ft

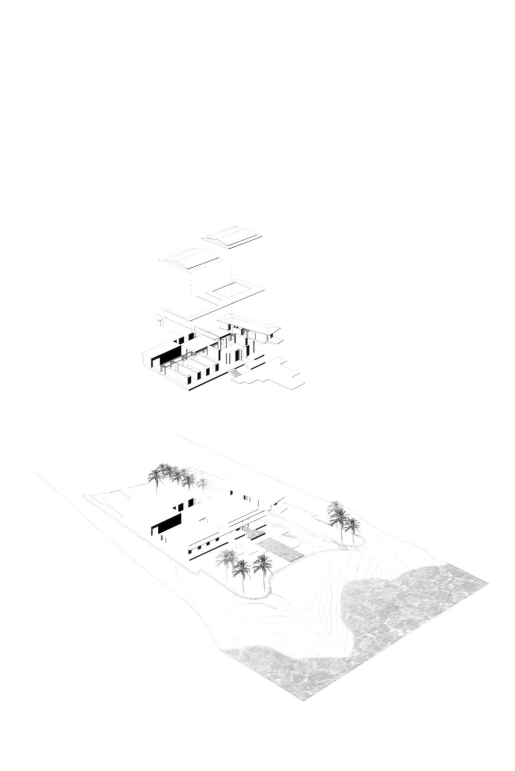

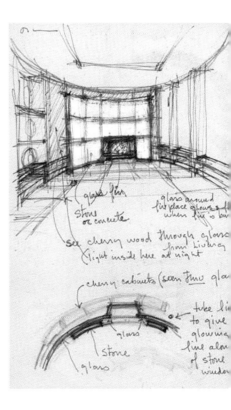

GLASS APARTMENT

The owner's collection of glass sculpture and the sweeping view over Elliott Bay inspired this fluid sequence of spacious and intimate rooms on the fourth story of a five-story condominium block. Kiln-melted glass was pressed over metal forms to make floor-to-ceiling translucent, curving partitions. Light travels freely through the rooms, stopping only at the dark, oak-paneled study. The white palette reflects and diffuses the natural illumination, glowing like the famous oyster light of the Northwest.

The translucent wall panels, crafted by artist Peter David, serve as a backdrop for the organic forms of multicolored glass bowls and sculptures by Dale Chihuly, William Morris, and other Northwest artists. Complementing these fragile treasures are paintings from the region. Display shelving is integrated with the cast-glass partitions, providing seamless and tactile surfaces that seem to float above the ground. Venetian plaster walls mimic the look of surf-washed pebbles; textured concrete floors evoke a beach. The spare wood and metal furnishings, such as the "lily pad" table with a weathered cross section of tree trunk mounted atop a glass base, respond to the large- and small-scale artworks.

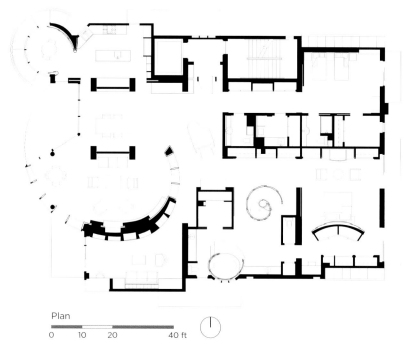

Plan

0   10   20   40 ft

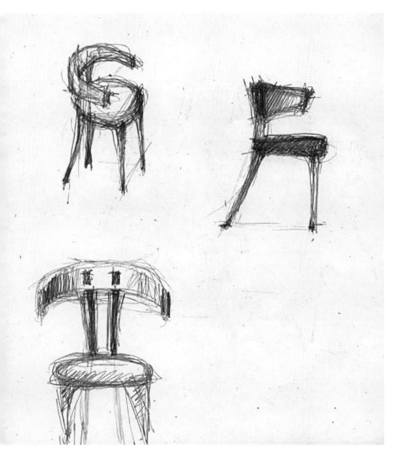

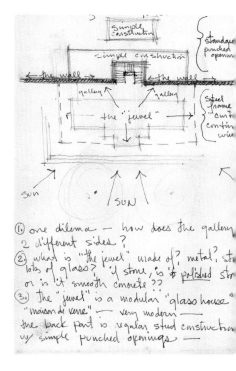

DECORATIVE ARTS HOUSE | **CENTRAL COLORADO** 2008

Large but simple and symmetrical, this house is designed for entertaining and the display of artworks. The owners needed high-ceilinged spaces in which to present large canvases by Colorado painter Vance Kirkland, as well as their collection of twentieth-century decorative arts. Local design ordinances mandated a pitched roof, even though the house is located on a sizeable wooded site, but the facades of stone, metal, and glass are unabashedly modern in character.

A two-story central gallery divides the public areas from the private spaces. The public rooms face south to a landscape of native grasses that evoke the eastern plains of Colorado. To the north, behind a permeable stone wall, are the owners' offices, kitchen, and other functional areas; these look out to a densely planted garden inspired by Colorado's mountain landscapes. The bedrooms are on the second level. The intense natural light is filtered through an exterior steel sunshade and trellis and is further softened by a translucent scrim under the skylight in the central gallery, which balances the light from the expansive glazing on the south facade. Newly designed furniture sets off classic pieces by Gio Ponti, Josef Hoffmann, Charles Rennie Mackintosh, and Frank Lloyd Wright.

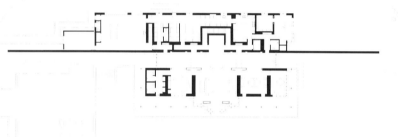

Plan

0   20   40   80 ft

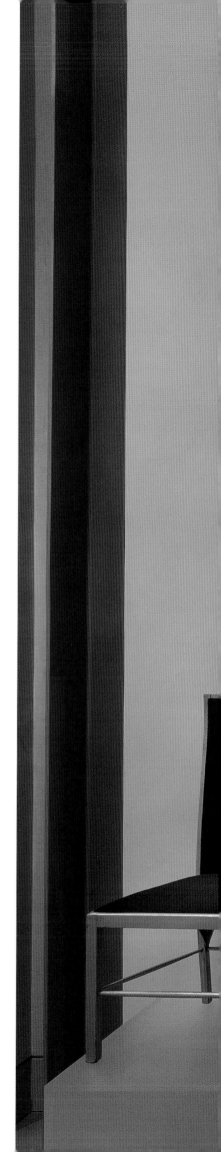

HONG KONG VILLA | **SHEK-O, HONG KONG, CHINA** 2008

Overlooking the South China Sea near Shek-O, a historic fishing village in the southeast corner of Hong Kong Island, this single-story house is designed to embrace the stunning coastal scenery. The site offers views in every direction, and the plan focuses views toward the cardinal points of north, east, south, and west. Concrete, stone, and glass, with metal columns and details, are employed to withstand the climatic extremes. Roof planes admit natural light while providing ample shelter from sun and driving tropical rains.

The house is uncompromisingly modern in its architectural language, but it is built around a large central courtyard in the traditional Chinese way. The court leads to a lofty rotunda at the center of the house and then out to a reflecting pool that runs along the edge of the sloping property on the ocean side, blending with the watery scenery. Steps lead down the incline to anchor the house in the natural landscape. The central axis and broad stretches of glass draw the eye through the house to the sky and the island-studded coastline. Flanking the dramatic central space are intimate seating and dining areas; private areas are located at either end of the house. Artist Mary Ann Peters painted a mural that spans the length of the house.

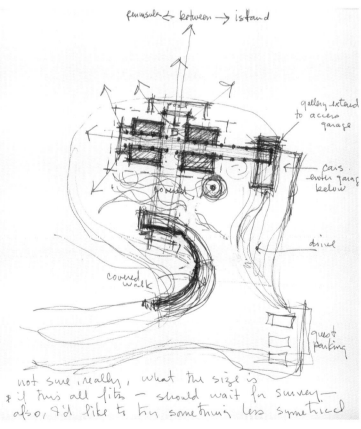

peninsula ← between → island

gallery extend
to access
garage

cars.
enter garage
below

drive

covered
walk

guest
parking

not sure really, what the size is
+ if this all fits — should wait for survey —
also, I'd like to try something less symetrical

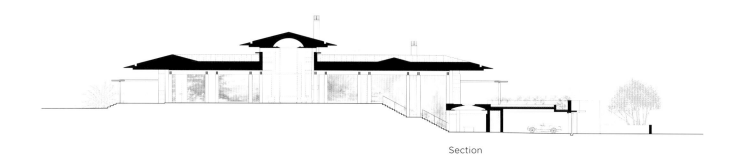

Section

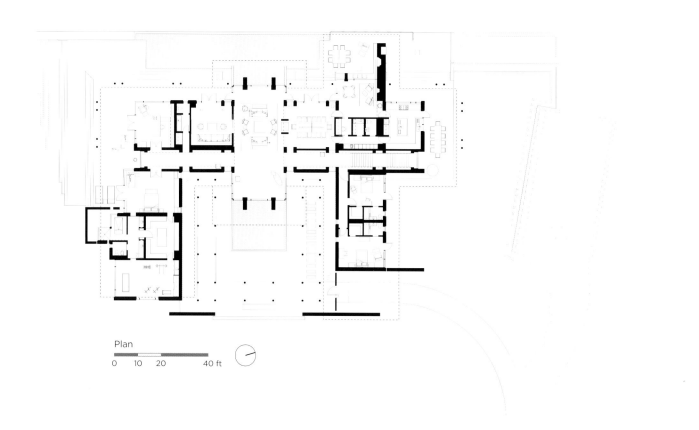

Plan

0   10   20   40 ft

OLSON APARTMENT | **SEATTLE, WASHINGTON** 1987, 2008

Over the past twenty years, my wife and I have remodeled and enriched a compact duplex apartment on the upper levels of a nine-story building in Seattle's Pioneer Square historic district. The apartment has served as a laboratory for exploring ideas about space, architecture, urban living, and the integration of art into everyday life. Built-in art installations by Jeffrey Bishop, Nancy Mee, and Ann Gardner extend and enrich the architectural expression.

The design manipulates the confined spaces physically and illusionistically. A twenty-five-foot-high light well links the two levels, dissolves boundaries, and pulls in gentle natural illumination from above. This focus on the interior balances the glass sliding doors off the kitchen, which open to a verdant terrace and close-up views of the city. The shifts of lighting through the day give way to serene nighttime illumination from ceiling coves.

An open staircase with a glass balustrade ascends to the upper level, passing a niche filled with contemporary art and antique artifacts that speak to each other in provocative ways. In 2008, the kitchen was enlarged and a sitting area was added. The opening at the top of the light well was increased in size; a translucent wall enhances the level of illumination throughout the apartment.

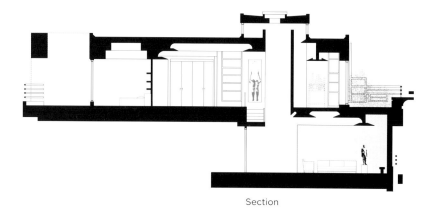

Section

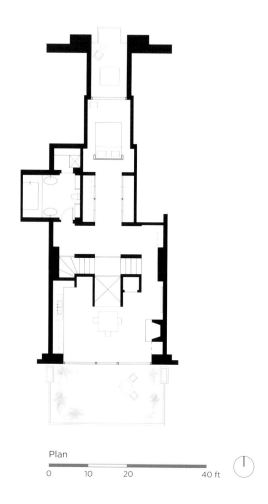

Plan

0   10   20   40 ft

JIM OLSON FAIA

A graduate of the University of Washington, Jim Olson established his own firm in Seattle in 1966. Since that time the office has grown into a diverse practice with an international reputation, becoming Olson/ Walker Architects in 1971, Olson Sundberg Architects in 1985, and Olson Sundberg Kundig Allen Architects in 2000. The firm is the recipient of the 2009 AIA Architecture Firm Award, and Olson is the recipient of the 2007 Seattle AIA Medal of Honor.

Throughout his career, in both residential and institutional projects, Olson has explored the interplay between art and architecture. He has often acted as a curator, selecting and commissioning artworks, and he has lectured throughout the United States and Mexico on the implicit partnership of architecture and art. In addition, Olson has focused on the relationship of a building to its context, whether natural or urban. His mixed-use Pike & Virginia Building, the first new building in Pike Place Market in fifty years, originated a method of fitting modern architecture into historic neighborhoods.

Olson has served on the boards of a number of Northwest arts organizations and community institutions, and he is an honorary board member for the Seattle Art Museum. His work has been published widely in books and journals, including *Architecture, Art and Craft: Olson Sundberg Kundig Allen Architects* and *Art + Architecture: The Ebsworth Collection and Residence*.

OPPOSITE
first row: BAJA RESIDENCE, Baja Peninsula, Mexico, 2010
EARTH HOUSE, Longbranch, Washington, 1969
second row: GARDEN HOUSE, Atherton, California, 1998
PIKE & VIRGINIA BUILDING, Seattle, Washington, 1978
third row: RED HOUSE, Denver, Colorado, 1998
NOAH'S ARK EXHIBIT, Skirball Cultural Center, Los Angeles, California, 2007
fourth row: ST. MARK'S CATHEDRAL RENOVATION, Seattle, Washington, 1997
WHATCOM MUSEUM, Bellingham, Washington, 2009

PROJECT CREDITS

OLSON CABIN
Longbranch, Washington
1959, 1981, 1997, 2003
Project Team: Jim Olson (design principal),
Ellen Cecil (project manager), Derek Santo
Interior Design: Olson Sundberg Kundig Allen
Architects: Jim Olson (design principal)
Selected Arts and Decorative Arts: Bedroom:
Bella Olson, Piper Olson, Jim Olson;
Deck: Jim Olson (chair design)
Consultants: Monte Clark Engineering
(structural engineering)
Contractors: Tom Harris (1981),
Mark Ambler (2003)
Photography: Benjamin Benschneider, Jim Olson,
Peter Yates

DESERT HOUSE
Rancho Mirage, California
1999
Project Team: Jim Olson (design principal),
Matthew Stannard (project manager),
Kevin Kudo-King, Motomi Kudo-King,
Katie Popolow, Janice Wettstone
Interior Design: Terry Hunziker
Landscape Design: Wayne Carlton Connor
& Associates
Craftsperson/Artist: Dan Daley, glass tiles for front
door
Selected Arts and Decorative Arts: Dining room:
Nicholas Africano
Consultants: Monte Clark Engineering
(structural engineering), Organized Designs
by Maxine (storage design)
Contractor: Stoker Construction
Photography: Cindy Anderson, Tim Maloney,
Dominique Vorillon

ZEN HOUSE
Seattle, Washington
1999
Project Team: Jim Olson (design principal),
Jim Conti, Stephen Yamada-Heidner (project
managers), Brooks Brainard, Kelly Brooks
Interior Design: Janice Viekman
Landscape Design: Allworth Nussbaum
Selected Arts and Decorative Arts: Gallery:
Mary Ann Peters (mural), Jim Olson with Peter
David (glass sculpture); Living room: Betsy Eby
Contractor: Charter Construction
Photography: Tim Bies, Eduardo Calderon

LAKE HOUSE
Mercer Island, Washington
2004
Project Team: Jim Olson (design principal),
Stephen Yamada-Heidner (associate), Jill Rerucha
(project manager), Carsten Stinn
Interior Design: Olson Sundberg Kundig Allen
Architects: Jim Olson (design principal),
Debbie Kennedy (project manager)
Landscape Design: Gustafson Guthrie Nichol Ltd.
Selected Arts and Decorative Arts: Exterior:
Alexander Liberman; Living room: Ed Carpenter
(glass light sculpture), Bernard Reder;
Sitting area: James Nowak
Consultants: Monte Clark Engineering (structural
engineering), Keen Engineering (mechanical
engineering), Studio Lux (lighting design)
Contractor: An Urban Company
Photography: Benjamin Benschneider, Tim Bies,
Andrew Buchanan, Eduardo Calderon

BIRD WATCHERS' HOUSE
Maple Valley, Washington
2002
Project Team: Jim Olson (design principal),
David Day, Shane Lowe (project managers),
Kelly Brooks (job captain)
Landscape Design: Belt Collins
Selected Arts and Decorative Arts: Exterior:
Philip McCracken (bronze sculpture entry wall)
Consultants: Robert Foley & Associates Inc.
(civil engineering), KPFF Consulting Engineers
(structural engineering), Franklin Engineering
(mechanical engineering), dePelecyn studio
(lighting design), Pro-Comm (electrical layout)
Contractor: D. Boone Construction
Photography: Tim Bies, Paul Warchol

MODERN ANTEBELLUM HOUSE
Atlanta, Georgia
2004
Project Team: Jim Olson (design principal),
Robert Jakubik (associate), Carter Woollen
(project manager), Elizabeth Bianchi Conklin
Interior Design: Terry Hunziker
Landscape Design: Ellis Landesign
Selected Arts and Decorative Arts: Entry:
Deborah Butterfield, Manuel Neri; Exterior:
Jun Kaneko; Living room: Todd Murphy
Consultants: PCS Structural (structural
engineering), Studio Lux (lighting design)
Contractor: Malone Construction
Photography: Bruce Van Inwegen, Scott Jenke

AN AMERICAN PLACE
Seattle, Washington
2004
Project Team: Jim Olson (design principal),
Stephen Yamada-Heidner (associate),
Peter Brunner (project manager/architect),
Martha Rogers (team captain), Misun Chung
Gerrick, Shiki Huangyutitham, Olivier Landa,
Shane Lowe, Jonathan Walston, Steven Wood;
Rick Sundberg (advisor)
Interior Design: Terry Hunziker
Landscape Design: Allworth Nussbaum
Selected Arts and Decorative Arts: Gallery:
Andy Warhol, Joan Mitchell, Gaston Lachaise,
Georgia O'Keeffe, Joseph Stella; Glazed gallery:
Marsden Hartley, Franz Kline; Living Room: Jasper
Johns, Alexander Calder, Willem de Kooning,
David Hockney; Family room: Walt Kuhn; Study:
Arshile Gorky, Edward Hopper, Gaston Lachaise;
Bathroom: Charles Sheeler
Consultants: Monte Clark Engineering (structural
engineering), Lighting Design Lab (daylighting),
Brian Hood Lighting Design (lighting design),
Coughlin Porter Lundeen (civil engineering),
Greenbusch Group Inc. (mechanical
engineering), Sparling (electrical engineering),
Organized Designs by Maxine (storage design)
Contractor: Holyoke Fine Homes
Photography: Tim Bies, Eduardo Calderon,
Paul Warchol

HOUSE OF LIGHT
Seattle, Washington
2005
Project Team: Jim Olson (design principal),
Stephen Yamada-Heidner, Kevin Kudo-King
(project managers), Dan Wilson (project architect),
Martha Rogers, Atsuko Mori, Steven Wood, John
Mrozek, Carsten Stinn, Tracy Margel, William
Franklin, Kelly Brooks
Interior Design: Terry Hunziker
Landscape Design: Charles Anderson
Landscape Architecture
Craftsperson/Artist: Gulassa (front door)
Selected Arts and Decorative Arts: Dining room:
Hans Hoffmann; Gallery: Antony Gormley,
Martin Puryear, Willem de Kooning, Philip
Guston, Tom Wesselmann; Living room: John
Chamberlain, Anselm Kiefer, Gerhard Richter,
Huma Bhabha, Stanislav Libensky/Jaroslava
Brychtova, Sigmar Polke; Light sculpture space:
James Turrell (light sculpture); Pool: Dale Chihuly
Consultants: KPFF Consulting Engineers
(structural engineering), Interface Engineering
(mechanical engineering), Coughlin Porter
Lundeen (civil engineering), Associated Earth
Sciences Inc. (geotechnical engineering), Sparling
(electrical engineering), Brian Hood Lighting
Design (lighting design), Organized Designs
by Maxine (storage design)
Contractor: Holyoke Fine Homes
Photography: Benjamin Benschneider, Tim Bies,
Aaron Leitz, Paul Warchol

GLASS FARMHOUSE
Eastern Oregon
2008
Project Team: Jim Olson (design principal),
Ellen Cecil (project manager), Michael Wright
Consultants: Monte Clark Engineering
(structural engineering)
Photography: Tim Bies

TRANSPARENT LOFT
Seattle, Washington
2007
Project Team: Jim Olson (design principal),
Valerie Wersinger (project manager), Janice
Wettstone (associate)
Interior Design: Ted Tuttle Interior Design
Selected Arts and Decorative Arts: Dining area:
Tom Corbin, Kris Cox; Bedroom: Tom Bolles
Consultants: dePelecyn studio (lighting design)
Contractor: CMI Homes
Photography: Benjamin Benschneider

CITY APARTMENT
Seattle, Washington
2008
Project Team: Jim Olson (design principal),
Olivier Landa (project manager), Jacky Adelstein
Interior Design: Holly McKinley
Selected Arts and Decorative Arts: Gallery:
Julie Speidel
Consultants: Perbix Bykonen (structural
engineering), dePelecyn studio (lighting design)
Contractor: Holyoke Fine Homes
Photographer: Benjamin Benschneider

OCEAN HOUSE
Hawaii Island, Hawaii
2003
Project Team: Jim Olson (design principal), Kevin
Kudo-King, John Kennedy (project managers),
Shea Bajaj, Stefan Wong; Rick Sundberg (advisor)
Interior Design: Anne Gunderson
Landscape Design: David Tamura
Craftspeople/Artists: Stusser Woodworks
(cabinets), U.S. Starcraft (metal fabrication)
Selected Arts and Decorative Arts: Gallery:
antique Southeast Asian sculptures, seventh-
century Cambodian Vishnu figure (small figure on
stand); Living room: Thai eighteenth/nineteenth-
century standing disciples (sculptures at the
center window on west); Sitting area: Sean Scully
Consultants: Greenbusch Group (mechanical
engineering), KPFF (structural engineering),
Horton Lees Brogden Lighting Design Inc.
(lighting design)
Contractor: Metzler Contracting Company
Photographer: Jim Olson, Paul Warchol

GLASS APARTMENT
Seattle, Washington
2001, 2008
Project Team: Jim Olson (design principal), Jim
Conti, Kelly Brooks, Elizabeth Bianchi Conklin
(project managers)
Interior Design: Olson Sundberg Kundig Allen
Architects: Jim Olson (design principal), Debbie
Kennedy (project manager), Cristina Acevedo
Craftspeople/Artists: Peter David Studio (glass
design collaboration, fabrication, installation)
Selected Arts and Decorative Arts: Living room:
Dale Chihuly, Guy Anderson, Jim Olson with Steve
Clark (wood, bronze, and glass table), Jim Olson
(bronze and wood chair); Breakfast room: Flora
Mace and Joey Kirkpatrick; Entry hall: T. L. Lang;
Bedroom: Philip Levine
Contractor: Krekow Jennings
Photography: Tim Bies, Eduardo Calderon

DECORATIVE ARTS HOUSE
Central Colorado
2008
Project Team: Jim Olson (design principal), Tracy
Margel (project manager), Blair Payson (project
architect), Dan Wilson, Peter Brunner, Crystal
Coleman, Gladys Ly-Au Young
Interior Design: Olson Sundberg Kundig Allen
Architects: Jim Olson (design principal), Charlie
Fairchild (project manager), Chris Gaul, Sophia
Chou, Christine Burkland
Landscape Design: Charles Anderson
Landscape Architecture
Selected Arts and Decorative Arts: Gallery: Vance
Kirkland, Fernand Léger, Henri Matisse, Matta,
Barry Flanagan, Jim Olson (table crafted by
Heartwood, bronze chairs crafted by Gulassa),
Frank Lloyd Wright, Charles Rennie Mackintosh,
Josef Hoffmann; Living room: Alexander Calder,
Josef Hoffmann, Jim Olson (set of two coffee
tables crafted by Steve Clark), Archibald Knox,
Dorothy Thorpe; Vitrine: Christopher Dresser
Consultants: PCS Structural Solutions (structural
engineering), Brian Hood Lighting Design
(lighting design), Organized Designs by Maxine
(storage design)
Contractor: Saunders Construction Inc.
Photography: Erhard Pfeiffer

HONG KONG VILLA
Shek-O, Hong Kong, China
2008
Project Team: Jim Olson (design principal), Scott
Allen (managing principal), William Franklin,
Wing-Yee Leung (project managers), Shea Bajaj,
Brad Conway, John Kennedy, Garin Shenk
Interior Design: Olson Sundberg Kundig Allen
Architects: Jim Olson (design principal), Charlie
Fairchild (project manager), Debbie Kennedy,
Sophia Chou, Chris Gaul
Landscape Design: In Landscape Co. Ltd.
Craftspeople/Artists: U.S. Starcraft (bronze
pieces), Michael Homchick, Stoneworks (fireplace
installation)
Selected Arts and Decorative Arts: Entry:
Deborah Butterfield; Gallery: Mary Ann Peters
(mural); Living room: Jim Olson (wood
and bronze chair and coffee table crafted by
Heartwood), Terry Hunziker (chairs and
side table)
Consultants: T. S. Chu Architects Ltd. (local
architect), PCS Structural Solutions (structural
engineering), Tino Kwan Lighting Consultants Ltd.
(lighting design), Rider Levett Bucknall
(quantity surveying)
Contractor: Brainfield Limited
Photography: Kasyan Bartlett, Benjamin
Benschneider

OLSON APARTMENT
Seattle, Washington
1987, 2008
Project Team: Jim Olson (design principal), Tod
Heistemen, Rik Adams (1987), William Franklin
(project manager, 2008)
Interior Design: Jim Olson (design principal),
Charlie Fairchild, Chris Gaul
Craftsperson/Artist: FlyLo (metal fabrication)
Selected Arts and Decorative Arts: Kitchen/
Dining room: Jim Olson (dining table), Sonja
Blomdahl, M. K. Gruth, Ann Gardner (glass and
metal backsplash tiles), Barbara Noah, Rik Adams
(fireplace sculpture); Living room: Jeffrey Bishop
(mural), Nancy Mee (glass sculpture), Don Brown,
Michael Ashenbrenner, Robert Graham, Bob
Jensen; Stairs and second-floor landing: Jane
Hammond, Pedro Friedberg, Andres Serrano
Consultants: Paul Marantz (lighting design, 1987),
Brian Hood (lighting design, 2008)
Contractors: Jerry Fulks (1987),
Toth Construction (2008)
Photography: Tim Bies, Dick Busher, Art Grice,
Robert Pisano

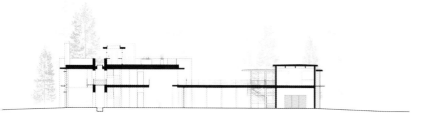